Faith on Friday

FAITH ON FRIDAY

A Deeper Dive

RIKKI SMITH

FAITH on FRIDAY

Faith on Friday: A Deeper Dive

Copyright © 2019 by Rikki Smith

ISBN: 978-0-578-54121-1

Copies of this book are available at quantity discounts
for bulk purchases.

For more information, contact:
Rikki Smith

Rikkismith@FaithonFriday.com

Printed in the United States of America.

Photo Credit:
Robert Jackson Photography
rljackva@gmail.com

Book Production:
Marvin D. Cloud, mybestseller Publishing Company
marvin@marvindcloud.com

Dedication

*This book is dedicated to former friends, who were my
constant companions: Discouragement, Anxiety, Fear,
People-pleasing, and Low self-esteem. You were with
me from the beginning, from my formative years into
adulthood. You tried to kill me, and tried to make me
believe I was worthless, with no purpose.
You almost had me. What you meant for evil,
God meant for my good (Genesis 50:20, MSG),
and I don't miss you at all.*

Acknowledgments

This journal would have never come to fruition had it been up to me. I was not ready, I was unsure, insecure, and just plain scared. I was plagued with so many "what if's." What if it weren't my time? What if it were dumb? What if no one liked it? What if I were overstepping my ability? Then I made the fortunate mistake of letting people in on what was spinning around in my head. Here's to not listening to myself.

Thank you, Toni Harris Taylor, Chief Training Officer, speaker, author, and coach of HARPO Enterprises, Inc. She said, "Put yourself out there, you will be surprised." Your method of coaching me really took me out of my comfort zone. I told you, "I didn't want anyone to see me." Look at me now. Coaching works.

Aisha Mack, my precious young friend. When I told you what I was doing, and that I didn't have a name for it, you who said, "Why not *Faith on Friday?*" And so, it is. Thank you for being creative and for being willing to share it. Oh, and it's time for you to blind the world with your brilliance. Don't make us wait forever.

Thank you to the many friends who have helped me, encouraged me, prayed me through, and who wouldn't come to my pity parties. Without your love and support, I would be curled up in the fetal position, sucking my thumb, and crying. I love you all.

To my family: Fredrick, Trey, Priscilla, Troy, Jordan, Tameka, Elijah, and Patrick. There are not enough words to express what I feel, and "thank you" doesn't seem to cover it all. Just know that through it all; I am because of you...

$\mathcal{D}$ay 1

New Beginnings

A new year brings new beginnings. Many people look forward to the new year and all of the new opportunities that are in store for them. If you look forward to the new year, but take with you the previous year's mindset, issues, problems, and drama, the new year will look a lot like the last year. What do you do? It is time to let some habits and actions go.

You must change your mind. If you want to change your circumstances that's where it starts. You must forgive transgressions, let go of trespasses, and put offenses into perspective. Don't bring the old drama from last year into the new year with you, then expect the new year to be better. That can be the definition of insanity.

Sure, some ugly episodes happened, some really hard times were endured, and some drama will leave residue in the new year. But it is time to take the objects that used you and use them for elevation.

You can build positive relationships, change and create a stronger mindset, and lean heavier on Christ because He can handle it. He knows all the things that you are going to go through already in the new year, but He has already equipped you to conquer them; you are more than a conqueror.

You must choose better, you must choose wiser, and you must choose to be stronger than you were before. Sometimes you must choose to take action although you are afraid. That means you may be doubtful, but you're going to do it anyway. Basically, you will look fear in the face and say, "I got this." This year will be your best year yet because you will change your mind and thereby change your direction. Remember, although we celebrate New Year's Day on January 1, your new year can start whenever you decide to make a change. Happy New Year!

A Deeper Dive

1. What will you not take with you into the new year?

_____

_____

_____

_____

_____

_____

2. What mindset do you need to change?

_____

_____

_____

_____

_____

_____

3. What new direction do you want to take?

_____

_____

_____

_____

_____

_____

"It doesn't matter who you are, where you come from. the ability to triumph begins with you. Always."

—Oprah Winfrey

$\mathcal{D}$ɑ𝒴 2

Be Encouraged

Have you ever needed encouragement and the people you expected to be there for you, weren't? Did people who come to encourage you, leave you feeling worse than you did before their visit?

Or my personal favorite: Have you tried to encourage yourself, but because of your struggles, drama, and issues, the encouragement doesn't ring true?

Let me encourage you today…there is nothing wrong with you. Everything you currently are, is exactly what you're supposed to be. Every place you're going is where you're supposed to go. Now what happens when you get there is another matter, but it's imperative to make a move.

You don't have to worry about what "they" are doing, what "they" will say, or what "they" will think because "they" have their own struggles and flaws.

It's important to do what you know you are called to do. There are people out there waiting for you to be amazing and fabulous for them. They're watching you and want to make sure that "it" is even possible. You're the one who's going to make it possible.

Don't be afraid. I'm not saying be foolish. Go forth and do great things. All that you have in you is everything you need to be a superstar. The problem is you seem to think you can't because "they" won't let you. As soon as you get up and make the move "they" will be right behind you, trying to do "it" too.

Don't give up on yourself before you have the chance to see what you can do. I promise you have what it takes, because He promised you can do all things through Him who strengthens you. Enjoy your journey, people are watching and waiting for you to get there.

A Deeper Dive

1. Who encourages you?

_____
_____
_____
_____
_____
_____

2. How do you encourage yourself?

_____
_____
_____
_____
_____
_____

3. What move do you need to make?

_____
_____
_____
_____
_____
_____

"Success is not final; failure is not fatal:
It is the courage to continue
that counts."

—Winston S. Churchill

$\mathcal{D}$AY 3

Put it Away

There is a difference between being a mature adult and being an immature adult. There's a Scripture that says, "When I was a child, I spake as a child, I understood as a child, I thought as a child: but when I became a man, I put away childish things" (1 Corinthians 13:11).

Many of us had a pacifier as a baby. It was safe, comforting, familiar, and at nap time, it was magical. It was also extremely appropriate for a child to possess. As an adult though, it is ridiculous, and needs to be put away.

How many adults walk around and hold on to childish and immature items? Envy, strife, rage, unforgiveness, fear, and bitterness, should be put away. In order to put those objects away they must be replaced with actions. You may owe someone an apology. You might have to offer forgiveness to the person who hurt you. Or perhaps you should find the root of your bitterness and get rid of it.

There are people waiting for you to grow up. They look for friends, mentors, coaches, counselors, and godly examples to follow. These are not assignments for immature adults. A mature adult understands putting away childish things is hard but worth it and necessary.

Remember having a pacifier as an adult is ridiculous; don't allow childish things to rule your life or trash someone else's life. Grow up and be an adult.

A Deeper Dive

1. What childish things do you need to put away?

_____

_____

_____

_____

_____

_____

2. What steps do you need to take to grow up?

_____

_____

_____

_____

_____

_____

3. What opportunities have you missed due to immaturity?

_____

_____

_____

_____

_____

_____

"The road to success and the road to failure are almost exactly the same."

—Colin R. Davis

$\mathcal{D}\Lambda\mathcal{Y}$ 4

Don't Quit

We all want to quit from time to time for various reasons: "It's too hard," "I'm too short," "I'm too old," "I don't have enough money," "I don't have the right people to support me." I get it. There is always a justification for quitting.

When we talk about purpose, passion, and God's plan, quitting is not an option. We have all been given everything pertaining to life and godliness. There are many tasks that must be done that only you or I can do. Changing our mindset is the best way to keep from quitting at the slightest hint of difficulty.

Get a mindset that says, "I must do this. This is important. This is necessary. This is what I've been called to do." Get up every day and choose to move knowing it will not be easy. Some days it will be downright miserable, but that doesn't mean give up.

Don't compare the end of someone else's story to where you are now in your saga. You may be in the middle of your book, going through hardships, struggles, and pain. If you keep reading you will get to the end. That is the place of testimony of power over pain. It is the place where you encourage others. The place where you win.

You aren't the first one to struggle and you won't be the last, but you will be the one others will look up to. You will be able to tell how you got up, kept going, fell down, and got up again. In the end, the battle is yours, if you don't quit.

A Deeper Dive

1. Why do you feel like quitting?

   _____

   _____

   _____

   _____

2. What is your current mindset pertaining to quitting?

   _____

   _____

   _____

   _____

3. What keeps you going?

   _____

   _____

   _____

   _____

4. How do you see your struggle helping someone else later?

   _____

   _____

   _____

   _____

"It doesn't matter how slow you go as long as you don't stop."

—Confucius

Day 5

Significance vs. Success

What is significance vs. success? First let's clarify that there is nothing wrong with success. Success is not evil. The problems come when we chase after success and do anything to obtain it. Success can be exclusive. It is often wrapped in "me, my, and I." People think it can be found in looking for the next job, the next raise, the bigger house, the corner office, the nicer car, and being invited to all the "cool kid" parties. If all you have is what's on your professional resume, you may be successful but not significant.

Significance is about inclusion. It envelopes "us, we, and our." To be significant means impacting and empowering others. This is seen a lot in coaches, teachers, and mentors. My 5th grade teacher, Mrs. Buffington, would not be considered highly successful by the world's standards, but she was of major significance in my life. Being a military brat I was always the new kid. I was quieter than the other children, and painfully shy. Mrs. Buffington told me it was okay to be new, different, and to talk the way I did (my accent was different, and my classmates made fun of me).

Mrs. Buffington told me one day something amazing would happen to me and I would be "someone special." To me, that was significant. She could have had a million dollars and it would not have moved me, but her words impacted me, and defined success for me.

Success though, can be lonely. After success has been attained, and we look back at all we have done to "get there" money, cars, prestige, and property may be the reward, but is it worth it if there is no one to share it with?

Significance will have people calling you, chasing you, wanting to be near you. Significance is what we should seek. It is your gift that will make room for you. Your gifting makes you significant by giving you the ability to impact others. Seek to be significant and success will follow.

A Deeper Dive

1. What does success mean to you?

_____

_____

_____

_____

2. What does significance mean to you?

_____

_____

_____

_____

3. How can you positively impact others?

_____

_____

_____

_____

4. What keeps you from impacting others?

_____

_____

_____

_____

"A life isn't significant except for its impact on other lives."

—Jackie Robinson

$\mathcal{D}$ay 6

The Journey

We are all on a personal journey as we try to find our purpose. Many components in life we do not understand. I listened to Pastor Rick Warren's series called S.H.A.P.E, an acronym for Spiritual gift, Heart, Ability, Personality, and Experience. I felt pretty good about all of it except for the spiritual gift part. That section bothered me.

I knew that according to the Bible, God says He knew me before the foundation of the earth, and that He knew me while I was in my mother's womb. He also said He knows the number of hairs on my head. The Word of God says God knew about me before I was born.

This stuck out to me in those Scripture examples. If He knew me before I was born, He must have called me something. I'm sure God is unlike my earthly father, who called to me and my siblings, "Hey you. You know which one I'm talking to." God had a name for me and I wanted to know that name. I prayed for an answer. One night I had a dream where God called me Envoy. When I woke up, I looked up the word envoy. Envoy means messenger. Then I began to search for the message. What was my core? What did God send me here to do? I am a messenger of encouragement. I found my purpose. Let me encourage you. God has a plan for you. It is wonderful, it is important, and it may be different than what you think.

When you consider God's plan, think about what makes you angry or what gives you pleasure? That may have something to do with your purpose. What is there about you that you tolerate and other people celebrate? Is there something you do that others marvel at although you think, *everybody does that*. It is up to us to find out our earthly purpose. The best way to do that is to ask the One who called you by name before the foundation of the world. Find your purpose and bless the world.

A Deeper Dive

1. What do people compliment you most often on?

2. What brings you pleasure?

3. What motivates you?

"The secret to success is to know something nobody else knows."

—Aristotle Onassis

$\mathcal{D}\mathcal{A}\mathcal{Y}$ 7

Don't Take it With You

The richest place in the world may be the graveyard. There lies ideas, unwritten books, inventions, gifts, and talents. Every coach, mentor, teacher and CEO ends up there. Everyone in the graveyard had something to be or something to do on the day they died. I'm sure no one had death on their agenda. The rest of their calendar no longer mattered.

What are you waiting for? Are you waiting for the right time, right amount of money, education, a certain age, or the perfect location? There really isn't any such moment. You are here on earth for a short period of time. Make it count. Don't allow fear to stop you or anything else for that matter. You have been placed here for a reason. When you start doing something or when you get involved, you can clearly define your purpose and your life's mission.

How many times have you heard someone say, "You can't take it with you?" Sure, all of those people in the graveyard left cars, homes, money, and jobs, but what they took with them to the grave was worth more than they left behind. Don't add more to the grave in death than what you leave behind for the living. There lies the apparatus that was supposed to change the world, feed the hungry, or heal the masses, but it was never realized.

You only have so much time on earth. Don't waste it waiting on the "perfect" time. Take this approach to your life: start where you are, use what you have, and do what you can. Don't wait.

A Deeper Dive

1. What have you been putting off?

   _____

   _____

   _____

   _____

   _____

   _____

2. What "perfect" scenario have you been waiting for?

   _____

   _____

   _____

   _____

   _____

   _____

3. At this point, what can you do to get started?

   _____

   _____

   _____

   _____

   _____

   _____

"Make the most of yourself by fanning the tiny, inner sparks of possibility into flames of achievement.."

—Golda Meir

$\mathcal{D}$ay 8

Are You Ready to Fight?

$\mathcal{E}$very day that we wake up and leave the comfort of our bed and the safety of our home, there is a fight waiting outside the door. I have a friend who is a big time MMA (mixed martial arts) fan. I'm not a fan, but I do like this about MMA fighters—each time they step into the octagon they know they are in a fight. They have prepared as best they could to take on their expected opponent.

Sometimes they must "tap out." Tapping out may look like quitting, but it is saying, "I was not as prepared for this fight as I thought. I'm going to train some more and I'll be back."

Are you ready to fight in your life? There are many opponents you must fight daily: fear, anxiety, hatred of others, and heck, hatred of yourself. You fight in business, at home, in school, and within yourself. Regardless of where, how, or what, you fight. Are you ready for the fight?

How should you prepare for a fight? First know that there is a fight. Do not think or believe that today there is nothing for you to fight. That's not realistic, and you will be beaten. Next, get involved with people who have already been in the fight and have won. They will have valuable tips for your training. Then, be watchful. Your fight can happen anytime and anywhere. You don't want to get caught slipping. You don't want to turn around and get punched in the face because you did not watch.

Your fight is real and it's coming. Be well-prepared. If you fight, you have the opportunity to win, even if you have to "tap out" to prepare more and return. Your fight will still be there.

A Deeper Dive

1. What is your fight?

    _____

    _____

    _____

    _____

    _____

    _____

2. What made you "tap out"?

    _____

    _____

    _____

    _____

    _____

    _____

3. What do you need to do to be ready?

    _____

    _____

    _____

    _____

    _____

    _____

"Opportunities don't happen.
You create them."

—Chris Grosser

$\mathcal{D}\mathcal{A}\mathcal{Y}$ 9

Be Quiet

Have you ever thought about the amount of noise around you? There are many distractions going on in our lives and in our heads. We must deal with jobs, children, bills, friends, and family. Much of our surroundings make debilitating noise within us. Where does being quiet fit in?

When is the last time you took time to sit and be quiet? There are sounds you need to hear that only you can hear. However, if you are busy being busy, or filled with being fulfilled, how can you hear what needs to be heard?

Some form of communication is being whispered in your ear every day. These words may deal with success, hope, joy, light, love, and peace. Because of the noise you can't hear them. Your mind works overtime to fix what you perceive as wrong. This noise may keep you from sleeping at night and from being your best during the day. What can you do?

First, be quiet. Find a safe place. This can be the closet, the car, or the bathroom. Don't take a phone, laptop, or tablet. Only take you and your thoughts. Listen to what is being whispered, the communication that has been drowned out all this time. Then write down what you hear. Don' try to interpret it. Get it out of your head and onto paper. You may find answers to questions that have been bothering you and keeping you up at night.

Stop being overly busy and stop filling your life with so much noise, that you miss what is being said in a voice that can only be heard in the quiet. There is clarity and peace in silence.

A Deeper Dive

1. What have you heard in your quiet time?

    _____

    _____

    _____

    _____

    _____

    _____

2. What keeps you from enjoying some quite time?

    _____

    _____

    _____

    _____

    _____

3. How can you carve out some time for yourself?

    _____

    _____

    _____

    _____

    _____

    _____

"There is a powerful driving force inside every human being that, once unleashed, can make any vision, dream, or desire a reality."

—Anthony Robbins

$\mathcal{D}$AY 10

Be Ready

Have you ever thought about first responders? According to Wikipedia, "A first responder is a person with specialized training who is among the first to arrive and provide assistance at the scene of an emergency, such as an accident, natural disaster, or terrorist attack." Among first responders are police, firemen and women, and members of EMS (emergency medical services). They are ready when the alarm goes off or when the call comes in. They are on the road ready to do what they know they've been called to do. They also know that the expectation is great.

What do they do before the call comes in, before the alarm goes off? Do they sit around doing nothing? Of course not. They maintain vehicles and equipment, hone their skills, read, and practice, because they know the call is coming.

It is the same thing with you. What do you want to be or do? Are you looking forward to becoming a public speaker, hoping for a promotion, or do you want to teach or change professions? What are you doing in the meantime? How are you being prepared? Do you put in your time and pay your dues? Are you preparing for the call that is coming?

If public speaking is your goal, you will want to be prepared before the invitation comes. Get some speeches under your belt, join a speaking club, and study what makes a great speech. If a promotion is in your future, know the ins and outs of the position, and get a mentor who will guide you along the way. You will want to be job ready before you walk down the hallway to your corner office.

Being ready takes time, resources, and commitment, but it's worth it when you know the call is coming. When the call comes and the alarm goes off, you will be expected to perform, and those expectations will be high. Be ready and you won't have to get ready.

A Deeper Dive

1. What will you do to prepare for "the call"?

   _____
   _____
   _____
   _____
   _____
   _____

2. What is keeping you from being ready now?

   _____
   _____
   _____
   _____
   _____
   _____

3. What is your next step to being ready?

   _____
   _____
   _____
   _____
   _____
   _____

"You know you are on the road to success if you would do your job, and not be paid for it."

—Oprah Winfrey

$\mathcal{D}\mathcal{A}y$ 11

Become What Scares You

Nelson Mandela, South African president, anti-apartheid revolutionary, and philanthropist once said, "I learned that courage was not the absence of fear, but the triumph over it. The brave man is not he who does not feel afraid, but he who conquers that fear."

We all have fears. Fear of heights, flying, public speaking, and spiders. What about other types of fears like walking into a room filled with people you don't know, fear of failure, fear of success, or fear of intimacy? These fears will either have you standing still or still standing.

Standing still says what you are afraid of has paralyzed you and you can't move. If you can't move, then you can't do what you have been assigned to do. If you are still standing because of that fear, you have found a way to combat, conquer, overcome the fear, and keep moving.

How do you combat the fear? First, determine what scares you and be honest about it. Secondly, assess why this makes you afraid. And finally, decide to become what scares you. Face the fear head on. You have a lot to do in life and overcoming fear is a step in that direction.

A Deeper Dive

1. What makes you afraid?

   _____

   _____

   _____

   _____

   _____

   _____

2. Have you tried to overcome it? How?

   _____

   _____

   _____

   _____

   _____

   _____

3. If you become what scares you, what would change in your life, socially, financially, and relationally?

   _____

   _____

   _____

   _____

   _____

   _____

"If you are not willing to risk the usual,
you will have to settle for
the ordinary."

—Jim Rohn

$\mathcal{D}$AY 12

Build Your Tribe

What is a tribe? A tribe is your "peeps, posse, crew," friends, family, and people who encourage you or who may be going in the same direction. We all need a tribe, but building one can be a challenge. We usually end up with a group of people who hang out with us with little to offer or bring to the table.

Building a tribe takes work. You need to be diligent about it. You want people in your tribe who are smarter than you, who will encourage and challenge you. You need someone to remind you to have fun sometimes, too. And you need a "shut-up" friend. That's the one who will tell you some of the ideas that come to your mind, should probably never come out of your mouth. You are either a shut-up friend or you need one.

Building your tribe is necessary to your mission and getting you to where you need to be. Not everyone can be a member, and not everyone wants to be a member of your tribe.

Do not be offended if you want someone in your tribe and they are not interested. Keep it moving. You will also be identified by the tribe you build. Look around you. Did you build the current tribe or did you keep the folks who showed up? If you are the smartest person in the group, you may need to add something to your tribe. Make the tribe what you have built, not what you have settled for. Everyone has something to offer but it may not be what you need.

A Deeper Dive

1. Who is in your tribe, and what does each one bring to the table?

   _____

   _____

   _____

   _____

   _____

   _____

2. Did you build your tribe, or did you settle for who showed up?

   _____

   _____

   _____

   _____

   _____

   _____

3. Is your tribe helping or hindering your goals?

   _____

   _____

   _____

   _____

   _____

   _____

"All progress takes place outside the comfort zone."

—Michael John Bobak

$\mathcal{D}\mathcal{A}\mathcal{Y}$ 13

Crappy Situations

How many times have you found yourself in what can only be called a "crappy situation" and settled for it? Perhaps you thought it was what you deserved. Maybe you believed it was okay or that it would be okay later. It's not okay. It's crap. You don't deserve it, and regardless of why you are in it or how long you've been there, it's not going to change until you change it.

When you find you have settled into a crappy situation you start telling yourself lies: "Well, I'm here now," "Guess I have to make the best of it,"and "I don't have any other choice." None of which are true. These lies are a way to help you cope with what you have settled for.

The first thing to do in changing a crappy situation is to recognize that the situation is crappy. Don't make excuses for it, call it what it is, "crap." Next, determine in your mind that you are worth more than the current situation. You were not created to have crap dumped on you. You are strong and powerful. You have what it takes to change any situation. Finally, make a plan. Take note of your strengths, your recourse, and your options. Write it down and make it plain, then work it.

Make up in your mind that you have the power to get out of a crappy situation because 1. You deserve better, 2. You were not created for this, and 3. It's holding you back. Get out of a crappy situation and help someone else get out, too.

A Deeper Dive

1. What "crappy situation" have you found yourself in?

_____

_____

_____

_____

_____

_____

2. What excuses have you made in order to cope?

_____

_____

_____

_____

_____

3. What can you do to get out of the "crappy situation"?

_____

_____

_____

_____

_____

_____

"Don't let the fear of losing be greater than the excitement of winning."

—Robert Kiyosaki

$\mathcal{D}$ay 14

I Don't Like People

Have you heard someone, say or even said yourself, "I don't like people?" Have you ever wondered what that means, or where it may come from? How can you not like people? They are everywhere. Even if you don't like them, you must learn to deal with them. Most times, this phrase is used by people who may not know or even like themselves. They may be people who struggle with their own inner turmoil: "I'm not social enough," "I'm not that friendly," "I'm not well-liked." And then you have those who really believe they are better than everyone else, or because of their "superior" intelligence, others can't relate. Therefore, "I don't like people."

The more you know about yourself, your strengths, and your weaknesses, the better able you are to get along with others, regardless of their social status, age, creed, gender, or any other preference. Dealing with others is a major key to succeeding in any area. Besides, how can you "love your neighbor as yourself," if you don't know who you are.

Take the short personality test, that begins on page 121, then answer the following coaching questions.

The more you know about yourself, the better you will be in getting along with, relating to, and being friends with others.

A Deeper Dive

1. How accurate was your personality test?

   _____

   _____

   _____

   _____

   _____

   _____

2. What did you learn concerning your natural strengths and your natural weaknesses?

   _____

   _____

   _____

   _____

   _____

   _____

3. How will this knowledge assist you in dealing with others?

   _____

   _____

   _____

   _____

   _____

   _____

"The secret of success is to
do the common thing
uncommonly well."

— John D. Rockefeller Jr.

Day 15

Me Too

I have spent time with some amazing people over the years. People who have started companies, raised phenomenal children, have marriages that have stood the test of time, and found their way out of hardships. I discovered each one of these people had issues or drama in their lives. Not everything was as perfect as it looked on the outside. No one is exempt from problems, pain, a past, or various other drama like scenarios, which brought me to this particular Me-Too movement. We have all been there, and no one is in it alone. You are not the first one to go through tough times and you won't be the last one.

If we are real with ourselves and others, there would be a lot less judging of someone else's issues. I'm not suggesting you run into the middle of the street and tell all of your business, but I am saying, stop pretending you have it all together and that your issue is too different for anyone to understand. Build someone up based on your shared life experience, and not tear down because of them. There is safety and healing in knowing that you are not alone. When you step up and say, "me too," help that is desperately needed can be found.

Challenge yourself to remember you are not the first nor will you be the last. There is no shame in asking for, and seeking support for what you may be experiencing. Stop telling yourself that no one would understand. It's not true. All around you there are those who can say "me too" and they are ready to help.

FAITH ON FRIDAY

A Deeper Dive

1. Thinking about your struggle, who have you heard of who has gone through the same thing?

   _____

   _____

   _____

2. How can you benefit from sharing your struggle?

   _____

   _____

   _____

3. How can sharing your struggle be a help to someone else?

   _____

   _____

   _____

4. How often do you say no one else would ever understand? Is that really true?

   _____

   _____

   _____

"Don't be distracted by criticism.
Remember—the only taste of
success some people get is
to take a bite out of you."

—Zig Ziglar

$\mathcal{D}\mathcal{A}\mathcal{Y}$ 16

More Than a box can Hold

Think of a ball. This ball represents everything you have been created to be. Every passion, project, joy, promise, and all the potential in the world, is in this ball. The ball is free to roll around, change direction, and do whatever it wants. In an open space, the ball is allowed to be what it can be. We have all been given the same space and opportunity. What happened to us? The answer is "Life."

In life we suffer loss, become disappointed, fail, and learn to fear. Because of those circumstances, we create a box to put ourselves in. The box is a place of safety and a place of comfort. We may call it a nice box, but it's still a box. A ball in a box is restricted of movement and can no longer be what it was meant to be. The box is too small for the ball because it was never supposed to be in a box.

You were not created to be in a box where you cannot maneuver, grow, or change direction. There are actions that must be taken that only you are equipped to do. But if you put yourself in a box that is too small for your potential, because of what life has inflicted on you, you limit your impact on the world.

If your potential is too big for the box you have created, it's time to get out. Get back into open space, where you can make a difference. There are people, places, and projects, that need what you have. By being stuck in a box, you deprive the world of your gifts. Get back into open space and ban the box. You made it and you can destroy it.

A Deeper Dive

1. What box have you created for yourself?

   _____

   _____

   _____

   _____

2. Why was the box created?

   _____

   _____

   _____

   _____

3. Do you feel you have outgrown your box?

   _____

   _____

   _____

   _____

4. How will you get back into open space?

   _____

   _____

   _____

   _____

"When you innovate, you've got to be
prepared for people telling you
that you are nuts."

—Larry Ellison

$\mathcal{D}\mathcal{A}\mathcal{Y}$ 17

Stuck

Have you heard of the La Brea Tar Pits? They are pools of sticky black natural asphalt that seep from the ground. It's a place where thousands of years ago, prehistoric animals would wander through, get stuck in, and become unable to get out. They would die there by starving to death. People have found fossils of huge animals that were never able to get out of that sticky goo, animals that never reached their potential, and were no good once they got stuck.

How many of us are stuck in a pit that we have created for ourselves. It may be a pit of fear, anxiety, our past, failure, loss, or expectations. Basically, a sticky, black pit that we are stuck in, that keeps us from moving forward. And like the prehistoric animals, we could die here if we don't get out.

People will walk by and see the potential you had that will never be realized because you found yourself stuck in a pit you possibly created for yourself. If you created it, you can destroy it. How do you get out of the pit that you are stuck in?

First, you must admit you are stuck. Secondly, you must determine what the pit is made of, and finally, share your need for help with someone. You may not have an idea concerning how to get out of the pit, but that doesn't mean the idea doesn't exist. Get involved with others and get out of the pit. You have much life left to live. Don't die by starving to death in a sticky mess. Get out and live.

A Deeper Dive

1. What has you stuck?

    _____

    _____

    _____

    _____

    _____

    _____

2. What is your pit made of?

    _____

    _____

    _____

    _____

    _____

    _____

3. What will you do when you get out of the pit?

    _____

    _____

    _____

    _____

    _____

    _____

"Try not to become a man of success.
Rather become a man of value."

—Albert Einstein

𝒟ay 18

Disappointed

When I was in junior high school, I wanted to play on the basketball team. I told myself I could do it and that it would be in the team's best interest for me to try out. I didn't listen to my friends and family who told me I should try something else. I also forgot that I didn't like to run, and I hated to practice. Imagine my disappointment when I didn't make the team. I was embarrassed, hurt, and couldn't understand why this happened to me. It took me a while to get over that incident, but when I did, I found out that I was a much better cheerleader than a basketball player. What is disappointment, and what makes us disappointed?

A disappointment is a feeling of dissatisfaction when a hope or an expectation doesn't manifest itself in your life or doesn't show up in the way you had envisioned. The reasons for disappointment are as varied as people. Some common reasons are poor planning, not thinking something all the way through, and being disappointed when that idea fails. It also stems from unrealistic expectations like when something looks one way in your mind and turns out to be completely different. For example, television relationships vs. real life relationships, and not knowing your own limitations like trying out for the basketball team when you can't play... (I'm still working through it).

What do you do when disappointment occurs? One option is to take the opportunity and get clarity about what is important to you, and what your goals are. Then share your disappointment with someone. You are not the only one in that situation. After some time (no time limit) you will find that growth happens, hope happens, and you move forward again.

Disappointment happens. It's all part of the human condition. Don't wallow in it, thinking that the universe hates you. Sometimes it's your turn to learn, grow, and share.

A Deeper Dive

1. How have you been disappointed?

   _____

   _____

   _____

   _____

   _____

   _____

2. What do you believe led to your disappointment?

   _____

   _____

   _____

   _____

   _____

   _____

3. What did you learn from the disappointment?

   _____

   _____

   _____

   _____

   _____

   _____

"In order to succeed, we must first believe that we can."

—Nikos Kazantzakis

DAY 19

You are More Than Enough

Who you are is more than enough. I consider myself a reformed people pleaser. As I grew up, I wanted to be a part of the "in crowd." I gave up who I was to be more of what "they" thought I should be. I ended up in places I didn't want to go, said words I was ashamed of, and acted out in ways that was embarrassing. That was a hard way to grow up.

You are enough. You are exactly who you are supposed to be and that's okay. You don't have to be what other people think you should be. Stop pretending to be someone you are not. You are more than enough. Who you are is what the world needs. Trying to please others is for their comfort, not yours. If others can mold you and make you, they can use you, trick you, train you, and name you. When someone else names you, they won't ask your opinion, and you may not like what they call you. Be authentically you. You have something to offer, and if you don't realize it the world will go without it.

There's a lot of work in being something or someone you are not. You literally must become a new thing. Why not be a better you. Sure, it may take some work as well, but it won't be as difficult.

Don't give up on yourself, instead give yourself a chance. Who you are is fine, and you will find that you like who you are better than what they want you to be. You are important, you are necessary, and you are more than enough.

A Deeper Dive

1. Who have you tried to be?

_____

_____

_____

_____

_____

_____

2. What makes you believe you are not enough?

_____

_____

_____

_____

_____

_____

3. What does a better you look like?

_____

_____

_____

_____

_____

_____

"A successful man is one who can lay a firm foundation with the bricks that others throw at him."

—David Brinkley

$\mathcal{D}$₳ɏ 20

Your Name is Your Brand

When I was a child, my parents would make statements like, "You're not going out of this house looking like that, not with my name." They were saying that the brand, our family name, has a reputation and my siblings and I were not going out to trash it by looking in a way that would bring harm to it.

What is a brand? A brand is a promise made to consumers by a company based on the product they produce. In the same way, your name is your brand. When you think of JC Penny, 7-11, Ford, Mercedes, iPhone, Android, what comes to mind? That is the same thing that happens when people think of your name. What does your name, your brand, say about you? Are you kind-hearted, funny, always on time, hardworking, or willing to help?

Or are you a gossiper, liar, hateful, mean, or untrustworthy? That is not a good brand. But it could be what you represent.

Your brand is important, and it's being judged every day. Someone is judging your brand based on how you talk, look, or the way you act. The representation may not be true, but it's truth to those who see it. Your brand, your good name is worth more than money. Sometimes your good name is all you have. When you're dealing with people, in some situations your brand can either get you in the door or keep you out on the sidewalk. Your name matters and you want to do the best you can to make sure it is represented well.

A Deeper Dive

1. What comes to mind when your name is mentioned?

   _____

   _____

   _____

   _____

   _____

   _____

2. How would you like your brand to be known?

   _____

   _____

   _____

   _____

   _____

   _____

3. Is revamping your brand necessary? If so how?

   _____

   _____

   _____

   _____

   _____

   _____

"If you really look closely, most overnight successes took a long time."

—Steve Jobs

Day 21

Why are You Sorry?

Stop apologizing for what you have. Many of us have great houses, wonderful relationships, drive nice cars, have high-profile jobs, or children on the honor roll. Why then do we look at these blessings and feel the need to apologize for them? Stop it!

You have earned what you have. You may have spent four plus years in college to get a degree, or you may have had to endure past negative relationships to find out who you are.

You might have raised children who were at times a challenge. Why would you apologize? You are doing yourself a disservice. The person you are, the accomplishments you have attained and sacrificed for, are encouragement to others.

It is a hard habit to break, this need to say, "I'm sorry," for God blessing you. The problem is when God expands your territory as he did for Jabez (1 Chronicles 4:9-10), people close to you may not understand. Close friends may be envious or jealous. Their changed attitudes towards you may cause you to say, "I'm sorry," instead of celebrating the blessings, benefits, and benevolence, God has bestowed on you, in order to put them at ease.

Decide today that you will no longer apologize for the achievements you have worked for. You have earned it and you deserve it. Stop apologizing for your blessings, instead testify to what you had to go through to get to where you are. Share with someone your trials, your failures, and your doubts. You have come a long way from where you started, and you have earned everything you have.

A Deeper Dive

1. What have you obtained that you find yourself apologizing for?

   _____

   _____

   _____

2. What did you do to get it, or get there?

   _____

   _____

   _____

3. How can others, struggling in the same area, benefit from your success story?

   _____

   _____

   _____

4. The next time you find yourself ready to apologize for what you have obtained, how will you stop yourself?

   _____

   _____

   _____

"The real test is not whether you avoid this failure, because you won't. It's whether you let it harden or shame you into inaction, or whether you learn from it; whether you choose to persevere."

—Barack Obama

Ɖ₳y 22

Your Bully

What do you think of when I say the word "bully"? Do you think of the child who is pushed down the stairs, someone being talked about, called names, or having objects thrown at them? What about bullying on the job? What about being bullied at home? What have you been taught about a bully? The most quoted advice is "the best way to stop a bully is to stand up to the bully." Have you considered you may be your own bully?

Think of the words you say to yourself, how you push yourself around, and keep yourself out of certain places because in your mind, you don't belong. Isn't that what a bully does? Have you stood up to yourself?

When you see someone being bullied, something inside of you wants to help, protect, or rescue them. Why then, when you bully yourself, do you not feel the same need to help, rescue, or protect you? You don't have to be your own bully. Stand up to yourself and say, "no more." Stop allowing yourself to keep you down, make you feel bad, or keep you out of places that may lead to your success.

The next time your bully (aka you) shows up, stand up and tell the bully "NO! You can't talk to me like that, you can't treat me that way, and I'm not going to take it anymore." Don't be your own bully then look for others to rescue or protect you. You must do it for yourself. Sure, we were taught to stand up *for* ourselves, but we now need to learn to stand up *to* ourselves.

Don't let your bully stop you or scare you from this point on.

A Deeper Dive

1. How do you stand up to yourself?

    _____
    _____
    _____
    _____
    _____
    _____

2. How have you bullied yourself?

    _____
    _____
    _____
    _____
    _____
    _____

3. Take a few minutes to talk to the bully
    within. What will you say?

    _____
    _____
    _____
    _____
    _____
    _____

"What I am is how I Turned out. No one is perfect and you just have to accept your flaws and learn to love yourself."

—Walt Disney

$\mathcal{D}$*AY* 23

Boundaries

Nashville, Tennessee is the home of Nissan Stadium, where the Tennessee Titans football team plays. There are boundaries everywhere. Some boundaries are rigid; no accesses allowed unless authorized. Some boundaries are flexible; you can walk in and out at will, if you follow the rules. Nissan Stadium is committed to the boundaries they have set. The boundaries have evolved as the fan base grows, as the team wins, or as the stadium warrants. The boundaries are set to protect the stadium's investment.

There are all kinds of boundaries that you set for yourself. They may be physical, emotional, sexual, or spiritual. How committed are you to your boundaries, and what kind of boundaries have you set? If you don't like the way people are treating you, check the boundaries.

Are your boundaries soft? Don't merge your boundaries with the needs of others and then play the victim when the situation gets out of hand. Do you have rigid boundaries? You know, no one gets in, no one gets close, and you are in control of everything at all times, but you may be alone and lonely. Do you have flexible boundaries? You know what to let in and what to let out, but you also know how to change and merge as you grow.

Setting good boundaries will help keep you focused, balanced, and provide protection for the investment of your life. Being committed to those boundaries will keep you from being mentally, physically, or emotionally manipulated by others. Learning when to be flexible with your boundaries will keep you as you grow and have new experiences.

We all need boundaries. They are important to have and it is also important to set the right kind of boundaries.

A Deeper Dive

1. In what area do you need boundaries or better boundaries?

   _____
   _____
   _____
   _____

2. What sort of boundaries have you had in the past? Choose One.

   o Soft-Merges with others and plays the victim

   o Spongy-Unsure of what to set and where

   o Rigid- Nothing in, and nothing out, no one close

   o Flexible-Controls access, chooses what gets in

3. How have your boundaries been challenged? What changed?

   _____
   _____
   _____

"Success is not the key to happiness. Happiness is the key to success. If you love what you are doing, you will be successful."

—Albert Schweitzer

$\mathcal{D}\text{A}y$ 24

Your Self-Worth

A few years ago, I went to Las Vegas, and enjoyed myself to the fullest. It was the first time I'd ever been there. I visited the Cartier's jewelry store. I saw the most beautiful jewelry I'd ever seen. I was stunned. The sales clerk asked me if I wanted to try on a bracelet I admired. Of course, (duh) it was shiny, gold, with more diamonds than I'd seen on one piece of jewelry. The sales clerk took the bracelet out of the case and put it on my wrist. It was stunning, and I was positive that I needed to have it to make my life complete. The bracelet cost over $100,000. Immediately, I took it off, handed it back to the sales clerk and walked out of Cartier's. Guess how much the bracelet was worth when I left? That's right, over $100,000. It's worth didn't change at all by my leaving it in the store.

Self-worth is how you feel about yourself. Consider this, you were created by God because of the worth He put on you. You have purpose and a mission, and it depends on you knowing how much you're worth. You are worth more than you probably give yourself credit for, and surely worth more than others might think. It's important to know your self-worth, with the understanding that your worth doesn't diminish regardless of life's ups or downs.

Your self-worth needs to be just like a $100,000 bracelet. No matter what happens in your life, on your job, with your family, and yes, even in church, nothing can change your worth.

A Deeper Dive

1. What has made you feel worthless?

_____

_____

_____

_____

_____

_____

2. When have you felt like a million bucks?

_____

_____

_____

_____

_____

_____

3. Describe what you would do if you knew without a doubt what you were worth.

_____

_____

_____

_____

_____

_____

"A Diamond doesn't start out polished and shining. It once was nothing special, but with enough pressure and time, becomes spectacular.
I am that Diamond."

—Solange Knowles

$\mathcal{D}$AУ 25

Take Back Your Power

Most of us have people in our lives we want to help, or we want to see them do better. We listen to them and try to assist where we can. The problem becomes when that help turns into us being dumped on with drama that is not our own. That allows it to become our issue to deal with, instead of making the other person responsible for their own stuff. We find ourselves holding their drama bag. That steals our power.

It's sad when you become an enabler. An enabler is "a person who encourages or enables negative or self-destructive behavior in another." It teaches them that it's okay for them to treat you that way. Yes, they learned it from you. Think of it this way. Who would take responsibility for their stuff if there was someone willing to take it and deal with it for them? Why should they take the blame if you are willing to take it? That takes away from your desire to help others. You can't because you have tied yourself to a mess that is not yours. What should you do now?

First, give them back their drama. Make them responsible for their own actions and allow them to suffer their own consequences. Stop giving away your life force and power to someone who only wants to use you. Next, start taking care of yourself, and don't feel guilty about it. Remember who you were before you became consumed by the piles of drama that took over. And finally, just breathe. It will be okay. Take back your power and be careful of who you allow to "dump" on you from now on.

A Deeper Dive

1. What drama in your life is not yours?

2. What keeps you in the middle of that mess?

3. Why not give them their drama back?

"Stop giving people the power to steal your peace. It belongs to you and no one should be able to run away with it."

—A. Elle

Day 26

Accountability

Accountability is the art of having someone in your life to help you reach the goals you have set for yourself. Accountability is not about having someone "in your business." When you are accountable to someone, you have expressed to them a desire or a goal you have set in areas such as health, fitness, diet, finance, or relationships. You have verbally expressed your goal to someone and given them the right to inquire about your progress. Therefore, you made yourself accountable to them. The next time that person sees you, they will probably ask about the goal. For example, "How is it going at the gym?" "Did you get the car you were saving for?" "Whatever happened with that person you were dating?"

Being accountable to someone is a great way to get to the place you want to go. You must be ready with an open mind to answer hard questions that may offend or upset you. Know that the one you are accountable to will not fix your issue. Your goal should never be more important to anyone else than it is to you.

On the other hand, if you are accountable for someone be mindful to stay on task. Only ask about the goal or desire, and not necessarily the details. Ask poignant questions that help them reach their goal, and make them think about the choices they will make to get there. Do not make them feel like they are being interrogated.

Accountability is a great tool to help move you forward toward your goal. Choose wisely, be open minded, and be ready to work at it.

A Deeper Dive

1. Who holds you accountable for your actions?

   _____
   _____
   _____
   _____
   _____
   _____

2. What goal are you constantly asked about?

   _____
   _____
   _____
   _____
   _____
   _____

3. What do you believe accountability should be?

   _____
   _____
   _____
   _____
   _____
   _____

"It is literally true that you can succeed best and quickest by helping others to succeed."

—Napoleon Hill

$\mathcal{D}$᚛ᚈᚔ 27

Choose Your Weapon

In a battle, it's not the fight that wins or loses, it's the weapons we use and how we use them. In the old days men would fight duels. They were fought with either pistols or swords. Never was a duel fought with one man having a sword and the other a pistol. That would not have made sense.

How many times do you fight a battle using the wrong weapon? A pillow fight is pretty tame, especially when you know the weapon is a pillow. When one person shows up with a baseball bat, the pillow fight becomes weird and deadlier than intended.

In your life's battle what are you fighting for? Is it restoration, dominance, or to show off? If restoration is the end game, then choose your weapon wisely. Don't overcome evil with evil, overcome evil with good. Don't tell a lie to fix a lie. Use the weapon of truth instead. In a screaming match, choose the weapon of silence. A soft answer will turn away wrath.

Be careful with weapons of mass destruction. These weapons will deliver a blow that nothing or no one can recover from. Shunning, withholding, physical or mental abuse, belittling, or demeaning a person are examples of weapons of mass destruction. These weapons may win the battle, however, you may lose the relationship, respect, or trust. All are needed to repair the damage after such a weapon has been used.

Therefore, if the battle is a water gun fight, leave the tank at home.

A Deeper Dive

1. What is your weapon of choice in a battle
    with others?

    _____

    _____

    _____

2. When have you used the wrong weapon?

    _____

    _____

    _____

3. What are your weapons of mass destruction?

    _____

    _____

    _____

4. Have you considered the outcome?

    _____

    _____

    _____

"There are people who don't deserve your kindness, be kind to them anyway. Kindness is a great weapon for the wise."

—Gift Gugu Mona

$\mathcal{D}$ay 28

Commitment

When most of us think of commitment, we think of the temporary sort. Consider the gym membership you bought and used twice. What does real commitment look like? What does it take to be permanently committed?

In WWII, the Japanese employed a fighting force called the Kamikaze. These suicide pilots would fly planes loaded with explosives directly into enemy targets. They believed wholeheartedly in the mission. They believed to the extent they gave up everything, even their lives. Now that's commitment.

What do you believe in? What is your mission? How committed are you to it? To be "kamikaze" committed there are things you will give up. Objects will be left behind or fall by the wayside because of your commitment. Friends, family, television, shopping, and even sleep will be affected, but your commitment will keep you going.

Discipline is the key. When you are committed you will become a lifelong learner. Everything you know isn't all there is to know. Being committed isn't for everyone. Sure, it's in us all, but not everyone wants to do what it takes. Know what it will take and determine if you are willing to pay the price. Commitment is the key and discipline is the door. Use them both and go all in.

A Deeper Dive

1. What's your level of commitment towards goals?

   _____

   _____

   _____

   _____

   _____

   _____

2. What will you sacrifice to obtain your goal?

   _____

   _____

   _____

   _____

   _____

   _____

3. How can you have a "Kamikaze" commitment?

   _____

   _____

   _____

   _____

   _____

   _____

"Commitment is the little choices every day that lead to the final results we're striving for."

—Anonymous

$\mathcal{D}\mathcal{A}\mathcal{Y}$ 29

Out on a Ledge

A ledge is a place we find ourselves on when we are ready to jump off. We may be on a ledge when we are on the verge of giving up because we have decided "I can't," "This is too hard," or "Maybe I wasn't called to do this." Most of us have been there at one time or another.

I have found myself on a ledge for no other reason than I needed help and didn't ask for it. There were several people who would have come to my rescue had I asked. I was ready to jump and no one knew I was out there. I had to encourage myself and talk myself off the ledge I put myself on. It wasn't easy. I had to get over my pride, anxiety, and fear. I was able to get off the ledge. At least that time.

How many times have you been out on a ledge of your own making and did not ask for the help you needed? How many times did no one know you were out there? When you are on a ledge, you have three choices: stay out there, crawl back in, or jump. To stay out there speaks to your inability to make a decision. Jumping means giving up and taking the easy way out and leaving others to "pick up the pieces." To crawl back in means you find a way to cope.

When you crawl back in there is a power inside you that says, "You can do this. You are not finished yet. You are good enough, and no one does it better than you." Crawling back in reminds you that others depend on you. Although it's hard, you have what it takes to make it.

Don't jump. There will always be ledges in your life, and you may find yourself on one. If you will not ask for help, and no one knows you need it, be prepared to help yourself. Crawl back in.

A Deeper Dive

1. What ledge are you on?

   _____

   _____

   _____

   _____

   _____

   _____

2. Why do you not ask for the help you need?

   _____

   _____

   _____

   _____

   _____

   _____

3. What can you tell yourself to keep from quitting?

   _____

   _____

   _____

   _____

   _____

   _____

"Asking for help isn't weak, it's a great example of how to take care of yourself."

—Charlie Brown

$\mathcal{D}\mathcal{A}\mathcal{Y}$ 30

This is for the Haters

A hater is someone in your life who wants to steal your dream. A hater is someone who wants to sabotage you, who wants to see you fail. It is someone who holds you down or pushes you back. We all have haters. Don't think everyone likes you. NEWS FLASH: everyone doesn't like you, everybody is not on your side, and not everyone wants to see you succeed. These are your haters.

Haters can be found almost anywhere: church, work, home, or school. Wherever you may be, you could encounter a hater. Why? Most haters are mad because you are doing something they wish they could do. Worse yet, they hate what you have: looks, job, talent, money. If they don't have it and they want it, they become a hater.

As you can see, a hater's problem isn't you. It's within themselves. It doesn't matter that they are in your face. The question is: what do you do with them?

Thank them for being a hater. You must be thinking, *Who would think to thank a hater?* Your haters keep you focused, keep you praying, and keeps you on your "A" game. As the saying goes, "Haters are gonna hate." Don't focus on them. Keep moving forward.

Identify your haters, then refuse to hand over your power. Having haters isn't all bad as long as you know they are out there and you keep doing what makes them hate on you. Remember, according to Romans 8:28, "And we know that all things work together for good to those who love God, to those who are the called according to His purpose." This means even your haters are working for your good.

A Deeper Dive

1. Are you aware of your "haters"?

_____

_____

_____

_____

_____

_____

2. How have your haters affected you?

_____

_____

_____

_____

_____

_____

3. What will you do differently since you know?

_____

_____

_____

_____

_____

_____

"Haters don't really hate you, they hate themselves. You are the reflection of what they want to be."

—facebookcovers.com

The 5 Minute Personality Test

On the following page you will find ten horizontal lines with four words on each line, one in each column. In each line, put the number 4 next to the word that best describes you in that line; put 3 next to the word that describes your second best; put 2 next to the third best word, and put 1 by the word that least describes you. On each horizontal line of words, you should have one 4, one 3, one 2, and one 1.

Further instructions and explanations are found on the following pages.

For example: One choice for the first line of words would be as follows:

_3_ Likes Authority   _4_ Enthusiastic   _2_ Sensitive Feelings   _1_ Likes Instructions

L	**O**	**G**	**B**
1. ___Likes Authority	___Enthusiastic	___Sensitive Feelings	___Likes Instructions
2. ___Takes Charge	___Takes Risks	___Loyal	___Accurate
3. ___Determined	___Visionary	___Calm, Even Keel	___Consistent
4. ___Enterprising	___Very Verbal	___Enjoys Routine	___Predictable
5. ___Competitive	___Promoter	___Dislikes Change	___Practical
6. ___Problem Solver	___Enjoys Popularity	___Gives In To Others	___Factual
7. ___Productive	___Fun-Loving	___Avoids Confrontations	___Conscientious
8. ___Bold	___Likes Variety	___Sympathetic	___Perfectionist
9. ___Decision Maker	___Spontaneous	___Nurturing	___Detail-Oriented
10. ___Persistent	___Inspirational	___Peacemaker	___Analytical
___**TOTAL "L"**	___**TOTAL "O"**	___**TOTAL "G"**	___**TOTAL "B"**

Total up the numbers for each vertical column (L, O, G, B).

Now that you've taken the survey, what does it all mean? Each letter (L, O, G, B) stands for a particular personality type. The column with the highest score is your dominant personality type, while the column with the second highest number is your sub-dominant type. While you are a combination of all four personality types, the two types with the highest scores reveal the most accurate picture of your natural inclinations, strengths and weaknesses, and how you will naturally respond in most situations.

The four personality types can be likened to animals to make them easier to understand and remember. Below are complete descriptions of each one.

L = Lions

Lions are leaders. They are decisive, bottom line folks who are observers, not watchers or listeners. They love to solve problems. They are usually individualists who love to seek new adventures and opportunities.

Lions are confident and self-reliant. In a group setting, if no one else instantly takes charge, the lion will. Unfortunately, if they don't learn how to tone down their aggressiveness, their natural dominating traits can cause problems with others. Most entrepreneurs are strong lions, or at least have a lot of lion in them.

Natural Strengths
- Decisive
- Goal-oriented
- Achievement-driven
- Gets results
- Independent
- Risk-taker
- Takes charge
- Takes initiative
- Self-starter
- Persistent
- Efficient
- Competitive
- Enjoys challenges, variety, and change
- Driven to complete projects quickly and effectively.

Natural Weaknesses
- Impatient
- Blunt
- Poor listener
- Impulsive
- Demanding
- May view projects more important than people
- Can be insensitive to the feelings of others
- May "run over" others who are slower to act or speak

- Fears inactivity, relaxation
- Quickly bored by routine or mechanics

Basic Disposition: Fast-paced, task-oriented

Motivated by: Results, challenge, action, power, and credit for achievement

Time Management: Lions focus on NOW instead of distant future. They get a lot more done in a lot less time than their peers. Hate wasting time and like to *get right to the point.*

Communication Style: Great at initiating communication; not good at listening (one-way communicator)

Decision Making: Impulsive; makes quick decisions with goal or end result in mind. Results-focused. Needs very few facts to make a decision.

In Pressure or Tense Situations: The lion takes *command* and becomes autocratic.

Greatest Needs: The lion needs to see results, experience variety, and face new challenges. He needs to solve problems and wants *direct* answers.

What the Lion Desires: Freedom, authority, variety, difficult assignments, opportunity for advancement.

O = Otters

Otters are excitable, fun seeking, cheerleader types who love to talk! They're great at motivating others and need to be in an environment where they can talk and have a vote on major decisions. The otter's outgoing nature makes them great networkers—they usually know a lot of people who know a lot of people. They can be loving and encouraging unless under pressure, when they tend to use their verbal skills to attack. They have a strong desire to be liked and enjoy being the center of attention. They are often attentive to style, clothes, and flash. Otters are the life of any party and most people enjoy being around them.

Natural Strengths
- Enthusiastic
- Optimistic
- Good Communicator
- Emotional and Passionate
- Motivational and Inspirational
- Outgoing
- Personal
- Dramatic
- Fun-loving

Natural Weaknesses
- Unrealistic
- Not detail-oriented
- Disorganized
- Impulsive
- Listens to *feelings* above *logic*
- Reactive
- Can be too talkative
- Excitable

Basic Disposition: Fast-paced. People-oriented.

Motivated by: Recognition and approval of others.

Time Management: Otters focus on the future and have a tendency to rush to the next exciting thing.

Communication Style: Enthusiastic and stimulating, often one-way but can inspire and motivate others.

Decision Making: Intuitive and fast. Makes lots of right calls and lots of wrong ones.

In Pressure or Tense Situations: The otter attacks. Can be more concerned about their popularity than achieving tangible results.

Greatest Needs: The otter needs social activities, recognition, fun activities, and freedom from details.

What the Otter Desires: Prestige, friendly relationships, opportunity to help and motivate others, and opportunities to verbally share their ideas.

G = Golden Retrievers

One word describes these people: loyal. They can absorb the most emotional pain and punishment in a relationship and still stay committed. They are great listeners, incredibly empathetic, and warm encouragers. However, they tend to be such pleasers they can have great difficulty being assertive in a situation or relationship when it's needed.

Natural Strengths
- Patient
- Easy-going
- Team player
- Stable
- Empathetic
- Compassionate
- Sensitive to feelings of others inflicted by others
- Tremendously loyal
- Puts people above projects
- Dependable
- Reliable
- Supportive
- Agreeable

Natural Weaknesses

- Indecisive
- Over-accommodating
- May sacrifice results for the sake of harmony
- Slow to initiate
- Avoids confrontation even when needed
- Tends to hold grudges and remember hurts
- Fears change

Basic Disposition: Slow-paced, people-oriented

Motivated by: Desire for good relationships and appreciation of others.

Time Management: Focuses on the present and devote lots of time to helping others and building relationships.

Communication Style: Two-way communicator; great listener and provides empathetic response.

Decision Making: Makes decisions more slowly, wants input from others, and often yields to the input.

In Pressure or Tense Situations: Gives in to the opinions, ideas, and wishes of others. Often too tolerant.

Greatest Needs: Needs security, gradual change and time to adjust to it, an environment free of conflict.

Desires: Quality relationships, security, consistent known environment, a relaxed and friendly environment, freedom to work at own pace.

B = Beavers

Beavers have a strong need to do things right and by the book. In fact, they are the people who actually read instruction manuals. They are great at providing quality control in an office, and will provide quality control in any situation or field that demands accuracy, such as accounting, engineering, etc. Because rules, consistency, and high standards are important to beavers, they are often frustrated with others who do not share these same characteristics. Their strong need for maintaining high (and often unrealistic) standards can short-circuit their ability to express warmth in a relationship.

Natural Strengths
- Accurate
- Analytical
- Detail-oriented
- Thoroughness
- Industrious
- Orderly
- Methodical and exhaustive
- High standards
- Intuitive
- Controlled

Natural Weaknesses
- Too hard on self
- Too critical of others
- Perfectionist
- Overly cautious
- Won't make decisions without "all" the facts
- Too picky
- Overly sensitive

Basic Disposition: Slow-paced, task-oriented

Motivated by: The desire to be right and maintain quality.

Time Management: Beavers tend to work slowly to make sure they are accurate.

Communication Style: Beavers are good listeners, communicate details, and are usually diplomatic.

Decision Making: Avoids making decisions, needs lots of information before they will make a decision.

In Pressure or Tense Situations: The beaver tries to avoid pressure or tense situations. They can ignore deadlines.

Greatest Needs: The beaver needs security, gradual change and time to adjust to it.

What the Beaver Desires: Clearly defined tasks, stability, security, low risk, and tasks that require precision and planning.

About the Author

Rikki Smith was born Rhonda Lemon in upstate New York, on a cold winter day in January 1964. Her parents were both in the military at that time and she enjoyed a childhood filled with love, laughter, and life lessons.

The oldest of seven children in a blended family, Rikki moved around a lot and lost her mother at a young age due to cancer. Nevertheless, God blessed her father to marry a wonderful woman who took the children into her heart as her own.

She was always the new child in school, because of her military upbringing. She was shy, quiet, and a little withdrawn. It was hard for her to make friends. She was bullied for being new, different, and for not standing up for herself. Thankfully, she listened to her family who told her, "It won't be this way always. There is more in you than you know right now." She didn't see it then, but hindsight is 20/20.

After high school, she went to college for one semester and decided it wasn't for her. She clarifies, "Okay, after being put on academic probation, I decided it wasn't for me. I went into the U.S. Army instead."

In the military, she learned a lot about herself, about life's ups and downs, and teamwork, but most of all, she realized she could make it. The military showed her she was more than she thought she could be, and her uniqueness and perspective was needed, to accomplish a mission.

Faith on Friday was born out of a challenge issued to her by a friend who said, "Just do a short video on any subject and put it out there." Rikki was petrified. She says, "I didn't want anyone to 'see' me, I had no idea how to record it, let alone post it, but despite all of my doubt, I did it. One thing led to another and here we are: a weekly video series, a YouTube channel, speaking opportunities, a journal being published, and a website. Not because I had a plan, but because God's plan chased me."

She believes transformational living is for everyone and anything people have gone through: life, death, marriage, divorce, disappointment, heartache, joy, and fear, makes them who they are supposed to be. She continues, "We are all a product of our life experiences. As I was told as a child, I now believe for us all: 'It won't be this way always. There is more in you than you know right now.'"

She now enjoys a full life that includes a diverse group of friends, reading, working out, and playing golf. She has been married 20 years to a retired Army veteran, and she is a proud mother to four adult children and grandmother to two grandsons. She concludes, "I am blessed, and I believe the best is yet to come."

E-mail: Rikkismith@FaithonFriday.com

LinkedIn: Rikki Smith

Instagram: rikkiSmith10

Twitter: RikkBat